Wha

By the end of this book, you will be able to read a company's financial statements and apply the basic accounting concepts underlying these statements. This will help you to understand the profitability of the company you work for and assist you in deciding which companies might be right for you to invest in. So read on . . .

HOW TO READ FINANCIAL STATEMENTS

Donald H. Weiss

amacom

American Management Association

*This book is available at a special
discount when ordered in bulk quantities.
For information, contact Special Sales Department,
AMACOM, a division of American Management Associat*
135 West 50th Street, New York, NY 10020.

Library of Congress Cataloging-in-Publication Data

Weiss, Donald H., 1936-
    How to read financial statements.

    (The Successful office skills series)
    "Easy-to-understand accounting basics for every
business person. Simple techniques for mastering
your company's finances. How understanding finance ca
contribute to your bottom line."
    Bibliography: p.
    Includes index.
    1. Financial statements. I. Title. II. Series.
HF5681.B2W464   1986   657'.33   85-28790
ISBN 0-8144-7644-9

Printing number

10 9 8 7 6 5

CONTENTS

Introduction—
Why You Should Understand
Financial Statements

If you've been reading the papers lately, you've been seeing a whole lot of this:

> Calling Ted Turner's offer "grossly inadequate" for the shareholders of one of the nation's most valuable television networks, the CBS board of directors unanimously rejected his hostile multibillion-dollar bid for the company. The network's financial adviser had deemed the Turner proposal "financially imprudent."

> Using an unusual leveraged-buyout technique, four Dallas investors acquired an aluminum-manufacturing company while sheltering debt service on the $40 million purchase. The investors created a corporation that bought out the manufacturing company—then liquidated the purchasing company, saddling the purchased firm with the debt.

> Unocal Corp. fought back against a hostile takeover attempt by Texas oilman T. Boone Pickens by offering to buy back more than 28 percent of its stock whether or not Pickens succeeded in gaining control of the company. The offer forced Pickens to "sweeten his bid" and simultaneously threatened to raise the company's debt load to intolerable levels.

That's the way things are in the business world—and things promise to go on that way for a long time to come.

Not a great deal of all this seems to mean too much to the vast majority of us; yet, as of this writing, that's what dominates the media. Not since the 1920s has financial news been hotter than any other events of the day, and not since the 1920s has what makes the financial news had such an impact on our lives.

Not just the national debt or the budget deficit makes the headlines, but commercial and industrial news as well. The stock market has restimulated the American dream and promises to produce the kinds of paper empires that once controlled Wall Street.

Wall Street has allowed millionaires to create these paper empires through friendly or hostile takeovers, through leveraged buyouts, through mergers. Companies fight back with greenmail and poison pills—methods used to buy up outstanding stock to prevent an unfriendly takeover.

But to most people, all of that goes on in the media, and it seems not much more real than prime-time soap operas. T. Boone Pickens—a real-life J.R.?

Some people buy and sell a few stocks or bonds. Some own some stock in the company for which they work through a stock-option plan or retirement program. Some even know what they're doing when they buy, sell, or acquire stocks. That is, some understand price-earnings ratios, debt-equity ratios, and other arcane words from an accountant's dictionary.

And some people work for one of a growing number of employee-owned companies—EOCs. When business failures in 1984 exceeded the number of business failures in any year since the Great Depression, a significant number of employees, to prevent themselves from becoming unemployment statistics, fought back by buying out their failing concerns.

In an economy struck hard by foreign competition, by artificial manipulations of oil prices, and by an enormous budget deficit that produced extraordinarily high interest rates and a huge trade imbalance, traditional heavy industries were hardest hit. Manufacturing firms and their employees reeled from one blow after another. Many ordinary everyday folk woke up one fine day in sudden need of taking a crash course in business finance.

Fortunately for Fred Fallon, a welding supervisor with ABC Metals, his reason for needing that crash course in finance came not because of impending disaster but rather as

2

result of his company's surging ahead. During the oil glut of 1983, when independent drilling came to an unceremonious splashdown in the sludge, ABC Metals changed its operations from oil-rig construction to commercial building construction—business parks, high-rise structures, and the like. After a year of struggling to get a foothold in the market, the company started to show a profit. Fred's moment of truth came when he decided to buy stock in the resurgent firm.

What a shock he suffered when he took his first serious look at the company's annual reports, something to which he had paid almost no attention before: the company's annual report and the 10K report to the Securities and Exchange Commission, both of which contained balance sheets, income statements, and statements of changes in financial position, most of which Fred had to admit he couldn't follow at all.

Who could blame Fred for gulping hard and postponing his decision? Go ahead and take a look at *your* company's financial statements. That's pretty heavy reading for anyone who might not have taken accounting in college. That stuff's enough to paralyze otherwise intelligent people.

Let's face it. How many people can read these documents? Writing a household budget seems difficult enough for most people. Preparing a personal-worth statement for the bank in order to buy a car takes an effort for which most people are totally unprepared. Even balancing a checkbook, for some people, seems to be a monumental challenge.

Well, I don't intend to teach you how to conduct a hostile takeover of your company—or even a friendly one. Instead, *I've designed this book to take some of the challenge out of reading the daily newspaper and out of buying a few stocks and out of reading your company's annual reports (managers' reports to the stockholders, management-control instruments, and the 10K report to the SEC).*

I've introduced you to Fred and ABC Metals only to have something concrete and specific on which to hang the concepts about which I want to talk. They are figments of my imagination and illustrate the most important financial documents any manager finds where he or she works. Those documents, though very imperfect in themselves, provide you with the most accurate picture of the strength or weakness of the organization. Without that information, you—as an employee, regardless of your position in the firm—have no way of evaluating the effectiveness of your firm's management team, and you have little or no control over your own future. With it, you might even exercise more control over the future of the company.

To help you understand the financial picture of your firm or of a company in which you're considering purchasing stocks or bonds, I'm going to explain the basics of accounting that form the foundation of all financial statements and four principal documents: *the balance sheet, the income statement, the statement of changes in financial position,* and *the budget of a management report.*

To impress stockholders and the public, a company's annual report often contains the subjective views of management as to the prior year's success and the prospects for the future, and it always contains the company's financial picture, along with an opinion expressed by the company's certified public accountants as to the fairness of the report. On the other hand, the 10K report, to which I've referred, contains the basic financial reports—*and* other financial details, such as inventories, depreciation policies, stock-option plans, and retirement plans. Required by law of all companies whose stock is publicly held, the 10K report is written strictly in accordance with the generally accepted accounting principles (GAAP), chief among them the principle of conservatism (about which I'll have more to say later). Since the chief executive officer and the chief financial officer of the company both have to certify the validity of the 10K, they risk severe penalties if they file false data.

First of all, please understand that financial statements have a language of their own, a language developed by accountants during the 600 years of accounting practice and codified into rules (GAAP) adopted by the American Institute of Certified Public Accountants (AICPA), and, more recently, by the Financial Accounting Standards Board (FASB). Then understand that, though the rules of GAAP often leave room for debate, the words accountants use make sense only because those rules pull the words together into meaningful

4

patterns for them. Those patterns then communicate a picture—albeit a sometimes inaccurate one—of a company's financial position. Yet even with all the limitations of an accountant's reports, they remain the best pictures available.

I will therefore start by defining some key terms and explaining some essential principles for organizing those terms. The Glossary at the end of the book will give you additional help with the language. Once you master the terms and principles, reading those financials that at first overwhelmed our friend Fred will be a piece of cake. Almost.

Chapter 1

The Basics of Assets

When you get right down to it, all those financial statements describe little more than *assets* and *liabilities*. They describe or explain *what the company owns* and *what it owes*, how it got what it owns and how it got into debt, what changes it has made in its ownership and debt, and how it plans to change its ownership and debt positions.

Since I'm starting with assets and liabilities, I also need to explain the report called a *balance sheet: the snapshot, so to speak, of the company's financial position at a particular point in time.* It describes the company's assets (available resources) and claims against those resources (liabilities and owners' equity) as of the date listed at the top of the balance sheet. A static account, the balance sheet shows only what is, not how the company got there, and it describes what is by listing all the company's assets and liabilities. A balance sheet for ABC Metals is shown in the sidebar on pages 6–7.

The *income statement,* on the other hand, *shows how the company got to where it is* (as described in the balance sheet). It shows income from sales and other sources, and it

(Text continues on page 8)

ASSETS

Current assets:

Cash	$1,000	
Marketable securities	1,100	
Accounts receivable	1,550	
Inventories:		
Finished goods	1,000	
Raw materials	1,222	
Work in progress	2,568	
TOTAL CURRENT ASSETS		$ 8,440

Fixed assets:

Plant, equipment	$8,230	
Land	2,000	
TOTAL FIXED ASSETS		10,230
TOTAL ASSETS		$18,670

April 30, 1985   (in thousands)

LIABILITIES

Current liabilities:

Accounts payable	$1,110	
Taxes payable	125	
Accrued wages	850	
Current portion of long-term debt	1,325	
TOTAL CURRENT LIABILITIES		$ 3,410

Long-term liabilities:

Long-term debt	8,450	
TOTAL LIABILITIES		11,860

Shareholders' equity:

Preferred stock, no par value— authorized 2,000,000 shares; none issued		
Common stock, par value $1.00 per share—authorized 5,000,000 shares; issued 3,000,000 shares	$3,000	
Paid-in capital in excess of par value	1,800	
Retained earnings	2,060	
Less cumulative foreign currency translation	50	
TOTAL SHAREHOLDERS' EQUITY		6,810
TOTAL LIABILITIES AND SHAREHOLDERS' EQUITY		$18,670

shows how much it cost to generate that income. The end result we call net income or (hopefully not) net loss.

The accompanying sidebar shows what an income statement looks like. As I go along, I'll explain all the parts of both the balance sheet and the income statement. Refer back to these statements as you read, so you'll see how all the various parts of the statements fit together.

- -

Consolidated Income Statement of ABC Metals
April 30, 1985
(in thousands)

Gross sales	$8,450
Less discounts and allowances	1,115
Net sales	$7,335
Less cost of goods sold	3,240
Gross income (profit) on sales	$4,095
Less general, selling, and administrative expenses	990
Net income (profit) from operations	$3,105
Less loss on sale of equipment	15
Net income (profit) before extraordinary item and taxes	$3,090
Less taxes	930
Net income (profit) before extraordinary item	$2,160
Less extraordinary item (loss from destruction of property as a result of an earthquake)	10
Net income (profit) after taxes	$2,150
Income per share before extraordinary item*	$ .432
Net income per share**	$ .430

Consolidated retained earnings

Balance, beginning of year	$ 360
Plus net profit	2,150
	$2,510
Less cash dividends paid ($.15 per share)	450
Balance at end of year	$2,060

*This figure is derived from net income before extraordinary item ÷ number of common shares outstanding.

**This figure is derived from net income after taxes ÷ number of common shares outstanding.

— —

Accounting Methods

We can report revenues and expenses in either one of two different ways—*the cash method* and *the accrual method*—and we can't ever mix them together.

In the cash method of accounting, we show only those transactions that have been completed—that is, those transactions in which the company has been paid cash for goods or services or in which the company has paid out cash for goods or services.

In the accrual method, we show income and related expenses as they are incurred—whether or not money has changed hands. GAAP recognizes the accrual method as the accepted practice, restricting cash accounting to very small, usually unincorporated, businesses.

Underlying the accrual method is an important principle, which I will discuss in more detail in the chapter on income statements, called *the principle of matching. This principle states that any income in a given period must be paired with—matched up with—the costs incurred in order to generate that revenue, regardless of when the costs were incurred.* If a company spent $450,000 in production in 1984 but didn't earn anything on its investment until 1985—when it

9

earned $1 million—the net income in 1985 was $550,000. The revenues in 1985 are matched with the cost of goods produced in 1984.

The examples I'll be using throughout this book will be based on the accrual method of accounting. That's the only accurate way of showing a company's net worth—which worth must include subtracting the company's liabilities from its assets, an application of the matching principle.

Assets: Tangible and Intangible

Speaking generally, *an asset is anything of value that is legally owned by the company,* whether tangible goods and/ or equipment, prepaid intangible items, or intangible rights. Assets are an economic resource of the company.

Goods the company sells are obviously tangible assets. What it gets in return for the goods are tangible assets. Physical properties of any kind—raw materials, finished goods, facilities, real estate, securities—are tangible assets.

Intangible assets also contribute to the worth of the organization. Insurance protection bought and paid for in advance (as is the case with all insurance) is an asset insofar as it contributes to the funds available to the company when the firm is liable for some insurable risk—injury to an employee, fire in a warehouse, maternity benefits, and so on.

We include accounts or notes receivable in the category of intangible assets because they're claims for sums of money due from customers or other users of company assets. We can even include patent rights to special equipment or processes—and copyrights on printed, audio, or visual materials—in this class of assets. Those rights can be sold or leased for cash.

You see? *Anything of value legally owned—that's an asset.* To decide if something is in fact an asset and what it's worth, we consider two characteristics: ownership and cost.

To own the item called an asset, the company must possess legal title to it. Leased equipment, leased property— those are not assets because the company doesn't have title to them. Their costs, in fact, are liabilities. Only if something is owned by the company can we call it an asset.

10

Assets: Current and Fixed

What we usually list as assets on a balance sheet includes a category called *current assets* and another one called *fixed assets.* Because they're listed first on the balance sheet, I'll describe current assets first.

Cash or anything that a company can easily convert into cash within (usually) one year falls under the heading of current assets: cash, securities, accounts and notes receivable, inventories, work in process, and prepaid expenses. We sometimes refer to a company's current assets as its *liquidity*—what the firm would get if it liquidated its current assets immediately.

Cash, also called cash on hand or cash in banks, consists of real currency or accounts in banks available to the firm on demand. The company wouldn't have to sell or exchange anything to get it.

Securities are nothing more than money the firm has invested in stocks, bonds, notes, certificates of deposit, and other instruments that can easily be sold and converted into cash. These sometimes show up on the balance sheet as marketable securities, investments, or short-term investments.

When goods or services are sold on credit, the amounts owed to the firm by its customers are called *accounts receivable,* receivables, or trade credit extended. Credit debts are assets because they're IOUs that can be called in and converted to cash. The firm can also borrow against them.

Another debt to a company that is called an asset is money owed to it, for example, as a result of loans it makes or some other activity—providing the promise to pay is in writing. Such IOUs—which we call *notes receivable,* notes, or loans to officers or outsiders—we could sell for cash as well as call in when due because they're negotiable instruments.

Another asset is inventory. *Finished-goods inventory* (also called merchandise inventory, goods on hand, or stock on hand) consists of anything of value that the company *sells* in the normal course of its business. Wholesalers and retailers stock finished-goods inventory. Manufacturing firms, on the other hand, also hold as inventory *raw materials* and *work in progress*.

Raw materials are what the manufacturer processes into finished goods. Whether the materials are really raw—such as metal ores—or parts purchased by an assembly plant, as is the case with ABC Metals, they have value for two reasons. First, they can be processed into goods for sale; or second, they can be sold as is. The *raw-materials inventory* is sometimes called simply raw materials, or material stock.

In addition to processing or selling off inventory items (in either category), a company can borrow money against its inventories. The inventory stocks are collateral, the firm's promise to the lender is that it will sell off those stocks and pay back the lender what it borrowed plus interest. That's *floor planning*. Many companies use this method to increase cash assets in order to pay off current liabilities—bills that have to be paid now, such as a payroll.

Work in progress is the other type of inventory. A company adds value to raw materials whenever it operates on them in some way. That's why even unfinished products are assets. We can sell them to someone who can then finish fashioning them into their final form. *Goods in process* and *work in progress* are synonymous phrases.

Service companies such as dry cleaners and the like that operate on goods that belong to other people have a similar asset that is more likely to be called *work in progress,* the work they've contracted to perform. Sometimes contracts for services, as in consulting, can be classified as work in progress, but the chances of service companies' floor-planning or borrowing against unfinished contracts are slim.

Finally, *prepaid expenses* are assets insofar as they represent resources that are expected to be consumed within a short period of time. Some prepaids are claims against vendors who have promised to provide services, such as executive search consultants, attorneys, or other professionals on retainer. Prepaid expenses are also referred to simply as prepayments.

So much for current assets. Now, *fixed assets are tangible properties or equipment that a firm uses to support its business.* We usually keep fixed assets for several years. We sell or trade these items, normally, only when they've out lived their usefulness to the company, or when we need to shore up our cash position or liquidate the company altogether. When we unload equipment, it's rarely at a profit, but we can make nice profits from selling property—especially in an inflationary period.

Whereas the categories of plant and equipment as well as land and buildings require little explanation, it might do to note that the exclusive right to the use of an invention or the ownership of a copyright is a fixed asset. That's right. That's because the rights to patents or copyrights are resources that have a useful economic life over a period of years.

The last item in this list of assets is called *goodwill*. We usually talk about goodwill as the way customers and other people feel about the company—the social attitudes or values created by the way in which the company does business. A cutthroat operation generally creates a poor reputation for itself. A company that does an honest and open business generates goodwill. Goodwill, in this sense, is the value of the company's reputation. However, an accountant can't measure the value of a company's reputation.

In practice, the accountant ignores the intangible value of "reputation" and measures goodwill as *the difference between the book value—the dollar value of assets minus liabilities—and the amount an investor is willing to pay for those assets.* For example, a company's book value may be only $75,000, but an investor might be willing to pay $100,000. The accountant, you see, is interested only in ways to *measure* the value of the company; he or she needs numbers with which to work.

O.K. For the sake of clarification, let's take the numbers out of the balance sheet that I've already shown you. In the sidebar on page 14, I've presented the bare outline of a typical assets column in a balance sheet. Read the terms and see how many of them you can define without reviewing the text. Then, go on with your reading.

The Cost Controversy

A basic principle of accounting states that we have to record our assets at their original cost until we sell off or otherwise dispose of them, that is, we have to report those assets at the

Outline of a Typical Assets Column on a Balance Sheet

ASSETS

<u>Current assets:</u>

Cash
Marketable securities
Accounts receivable
Inventories:
   Finished goods
   Raw materials
   Work in progress

  TOTAL CURRENT ASSETS

<u>Fixed assets:</u>

Plant, equipment
Land

  TOTAL FIXED ASSETS

<u>Other assets:</u>

Intangible assets
Goodwill

  TOTAL OTHER ASSETS

   TOTAL ASSETS

- - - - - - - - - - - - - - - - - - -

price we paid when we bought them. If the company traded for them, then the cost of the items equals the fair market value of the property or the rights we traded.

This cost factor causes many financial pundits considerable anguish—acquisition cost versus replacement cost.

In a nutshell, the controversy concerns what an asset is really worth at any given moment. Let's take as an example a piece of production machinery at ABC Metals—say, a stamping machine. In 1983, when ABC Metals bought the machine, it paid $20,000. By 1985, that two-year-old machine has suffered much wear and tear and has been depreciated for two years in a row. Obviously, it's not worth $20,000 anymore. And to replace it will probably cost $25,000, due to inflation and/or advances in technology.

At the same time it bought the machine, ABC Metals bought two acres adjacent to the land on which the plant sits—for possible expansion. It acquired the property for $5,000 an acre in 1976. It could get $8,500 an acre for it now. What, then, is the true worth of the asset?

For reporting purposes, most accountants apply the *principle of conservatism.* The general principle requires that you *understate your income and overstate your costs in order to control the potential for misrepresenting the value of a company.* As they interpret that principle, traditional accountants maintain that *you should record assets at their acquisition cost (adjusted for depreciation) and carry them in your financial statements at that price until you sell them.* That goes for inventories as well as for properties and equipment.

Other accountants argue that recording and carrying assets at acquisition cost distorts the true asset picture of an organization by grossly understating the value of some assets while overstating the value of others. The firm misleads itself and its investors with statements that don't reflect the real costs of doing business.

They also argue that if you are an investor, you really don't have a solid basis for judging management's performance. When the managers sell off part of the firm's investment, the resulting return is based on past costs, not current prices. Part of the value of the sale, during inflationary times, is based on uncontrollable market prices—inflated dollars. The real value of the investment and the return on it (the ROI) is hidden.

Revisionist accountants propose to change the convention by which assets are reported from *original cost* to *replacement value* in order to provide a truer picture of a company's competitive position *in relation to its present market conditions.* Status quo accountants charge that it's simplistic to think that one can accurately estimate the true, current value of older assets still in use. After all, how much is that stamping machine really worth today?

Now, I must have had some point in mind when I embroiled you in this somewhat esoteric debate. It's simply this:

When examining a balance sheet, the document that describes a company's assets at a particular point in time, you have to look beyond the dollars and cents to understand how the organization really operates and what its real potential is.

Chapter 2

The Basics of Liabilities and Owners' Equity

They say you have to spend money to make money. Unless a company operates its business on a strictly cash basis, and that means cash on delivery, it's going to owe money to someone, somewhere on the date of the balance sheet. If the firm doesn't owe someone money, it's bound to owe goods or services already sold or under contract. Those debts we call liabilities.

We divide liabilities into three parts: *current liabilities, long-term liabilities,* and *owners' equity.* Current liabilities are short-term in nature, payable within a year and usually from current assets. Long-term liabilities have longer lives, due after one year or more. Owners' equity refers to the value of the company after liabilities are deducted from assets.

Whereas short- and long-term liabilities refer to debts run up in the course of doing business (they reflect operating expenses of one kind or another), owners' equity is a special liability. What we call this section depends on the kind of company—whether it is a corporation or not. If it's a corporation or a utility, we can call the equity *capitalization or shareholders' equity.* Regardless, *this section reflects the*

*alue of the company to its owners, the difference between
ssets and other liabilities.*

I can make the idea of equity clearer by talking about my
ypothetical firm, ABC Metals. ABC Metals has total assets
vorth $18,670,000 and total liabilities of $11,860,000; then if
ne assets are sold off and all the debts paid, the owners or
tockholders will claim $6,810,000 for themselves. How
nuch that comes to per stockholder depends on the number
ind types of shares outstanding.

I'll come back to equity later. I need to describe short-term
abilities first, and then long-term liabilities in order to put
·quity into its proper perspective.

All liabilities consist of written promises to pay money or
rade goods or services in return for money, goods, or
·ervices. Or there is an implied promise to pay, as in ac-
:ounts payable. Whether the liability is a written or an implied
·romise, the amount of the cumulative debts appears on the
·alance sheet. Only the date of their maturity distinguishes
·etween types of liabilities.

We call debts the company expects to pay off after a period
·f one year *long-term* or *fixed liabilities,* which consist of
·otes (on money borrowed for operating expenses), mort-
·ages (on properties purchased), and bonds (pledges to pay
·rincipal and interest in return for cash). Bonds can be
·ecured (indentured) or unsecured (debentured); they can
·e registered (bonds issued to a specific individual rather
·han as a public offering), and they can be couponed (issued
·vith stubs attached for each interest payment due). No
natter what the type, all such debts are logged under the
·eading of long-term or fixed liabilities.

Short-term debts or liabilities, on the other hand, are those
·hat the company expects to pay off within a year. Called
:*urrent liabilities,* they consist of the costs of doing business,
·s in the purchase of goods or services from vendors or
·uppliers, taxes owed to state and federal governments, and
·repayments by customers for goods or services yet to be
·lelivered.

As you noticed in the case of assets, accounts can be
·eferred to by different names. It depends strictly on the
·redilection of the firm's accountant.

17

Accounts payable, for example, we can call simply payables or accruals. *Wages payable* is synonymous with accrued payroll or wages due. *Prepayments by customers* are referred to as unearned sales income, advances, or simply prepayments.

However, unlike the question of the cost of assets, the value of a liability is not in question. It's determined by the value of the transaction itself. If, on the date of the balance sheet, you have bills for goods or services totaling $100,000, the accounts payable will read $100,000.

Equity is also commonly divided into two parts: *capital stock* and *retained earnings.*

In a privately owned company or a partnership, capital stock refers to the money the owner or owners originally invested in the company. In a corporation, capital stock refers to the amount of money raised by selling shares in the company, which stocks can take three different forms—(1) equal shares, (2) common stock, and (3) preferred stock.

In some closed corporations, with no public offerings, there exists only one class of stock, with each share carrying the same rights and privileges. Usually, these rights include:

1. The right to attend meetings of the stockholders.
2. The right to vote for directors and on other matters.
3. The right to receive dividends as declared by the directors.
4. The right to inspect the books and records as appropriate.
5. The right to purchase any new issue of stock at a later date proportionate to the shares currently owned.

In most public corporations, with stock issued for sale to the general public, stocks are classified as either common shares or preferred shares.

Common-stock shareholders have all the general rights and privileges I listed above. If you'll look back at ABC Metal's balance sheet, you'll notice the reference to *par value.* In the past, that referred to the price of the stock when originally issued by the company. Today, the price is arbitrarily set at at least $1.00 or $1.25 to avoid high franchise taxes placed on the par value of stock issues. That's why the report also refers to *paid-in capital in excess of par value:* the amount over and above the par value that the company received when it issued the stock. (Note the similarity between paid-in capital and goodwill.)

Preferred stockholders have the privilege of having prior, or first, claim on profits or on assets in the event the company is liquidated, and they could have other special preferences setting them apart from other stockholders. However, those

---

Outline of a Typical Liabilities Column on a Balance Sheet

LIABILITIES

Current liabilities:

Accounts payable
Taxes payable
Accrued wages and expenses
Current portion of long-term debt

TOTAL CURRENT LIABILITIES

Long-term liabilities:

Long-term debt
Bonds payable

TOTAL LIABILITIES

Owners' (shareholders') equity:

Capital stock
Preferred stock
Common stock
Paid-in capital in excess of par value
Retained earnings
Cumulative translation adjustment

TOTAL OWNERS' (SHAREHOLDERS') EQUITY

TOTAL LIABILITIES AND OWNERS' EQUITY

---

privileges usually cost preferred shareholders some, if not all, of their general rights, such as the right to vote. (Notice that no par value is required of preferred stock, and though authorized, the company is not bound by regulation to offer any for sale.)

Whereas most balance sheets of closed corporations use the heading *capital stock* to refer to the cumulative value of their owners' shares, public corporations use the phrase *shareholders' equity* and clearly distinguish between ownership in either preferred stock or common stock, identifying the value of each type of stock and the number of shares of each type of stock outstanding (owned outside the company itself).

Equity is also stated in terms of *retained earnings.* In simplest terms, this represents the profits of the company from operations since its inception that have not been withdrawn by the owners or distributed as dividends.

In recent years, many companies have also adopted an accounting standard called *foreign currency translation.* This category reflects gains and losses on the translation of foreign financial operations into U.S. dollars from currencies in which business is conducted. Because of the strength of the U.S. dollar overseas, this item usually shows up as a loss under the heading of *cumulative foreign currency translation adjustment* or *cumulative translation adjustment.*

I've outlined the liabilities section of a typical balance sheet in the sidebar on page 19, just as I did with the assets section earlier. Here, again, you might want to stop now and review the categories to fix them in your mind before moving on.

Chapter 3

The Balance Sheet: Assets = Liabilities + Owners' Equity

Well, now that I've covered the jargon of the financial statement known as the balance sheet, let's put a whole one together. You will want to refer back to the balance sheet and income statement of the fictitious ABC Metals.

When you read that balance sheet, you see that the formula in the chapter title above holds true. In fact, that's where this document gets its name: a balance sheet. The assets must balance with the sum of liabilities plus equity.

(By the way, the format I'm using is called a T-account. Some accountants use another format, called a report form, which lists everything in one column. I prefer this style because you can see the balance at one glance.)

Now you're ready to take a look at whether or not Fred Fallon should buy stock in the company where he works, ABC Metals. As an oil-field—equipment manufacturing firm, ABC hadn't been making out too well, but now, with its new direction in steel fabrication for commercial buildings, it's beginning to do much better.

Read ABC's income statement and see for yourself. At the beginning of the reporting period (which would have been May 1, 1984), the retained earnings balance (near the bottom of the statement) was only $360,000. The balance at the end of the year (after dividends were paid) was $2,060,000. The difference between these two figures is $1,700,000—a 472 percent increase.

So the question is, what does all that mean? Has ABC Metals become a good investment, at least on the face of the figures? If I stopped here, would Fred have enough information to make a rational decision? I'd have to say no. Fred needs much more information before he sinks money into ABC Metals.

The income statement looks promising, but it's not a good place to begin his analysis. As a prospective investor, Fred has to put aside his feelings for the company. He's going to have to take a long, hard look at some tough numbers. Most of the answers he'll need come from ABC's balance sheet. That'll give him a picture of the net worth of the company against which he can relate its performance during that one year. And even then, a one-year performance picture may not be adequate either.

Some of the answers Fred will need lie in calculations concerning the assets side of the balance sheet. Other answers come from ratios drawn from the liabilities side. The tests I'll apply to the balance sheet are:

1. Leverage ratio analysis
2. Acid test
3. Current ratio analysis
4. Working-capital evaluation

First of all, what is the company really worth? If you look at the balance sheet, you might be inclined to say it's worth of $6,810,000 (the total shareholders' equity), or $18,670,000 (it's total assets). But when asking about the real worth of a company, you want to know whether or not it's able to meet its obligations—that is, pay its bills, fulfill its contractual commitments, pay its shareholders a profit, and so on. So let's see, first, since its debt load is quite high ($9,775,000), if ABC can manage that level of debt and still conduct business. To do this, Fred needs to find the *the leverage ratio: the relationship of total liabilities to shareowners' equity.*

When a company's proportion of debt to capitalization from the sale of stock is high, we say the company is highly leveraged. When a company is highly leveraged, and if it is highly successful, then it can still give a decent return on its shareholders' investments. The earnings per share can be maintained.

Since the leverage ratio measures the relationship between the number of dollars invested by shareholders and the number of dollars lent by creditors (loans and/or bonds), the higher the ratio, the lower the leverage. A high of 1.75 to a low of 1.0 is the range of acceptability for this ratio in the metals industry.

Let's take a closer look at ABC's leverage ratio, which can be computed by taking the total liabilities and dividing that by total shareholders' equity. As ABC's balance sheet shows, the company's total liabilities come to $11,860,000; shareholders' equity comes to $6,810,000—so the leverage ratio comes out to 1.74. In our business climate that proportion is common and acceptable.

Now Fred will have to see if ABC Metals fails *the acid test*. This test gauges a company's liquidity. It examines the company's ability to meet its short-term commitments—whether or not it has the ready cash or securities or other quick (liquid) assets to meet its bills and payroll over the next few months. Paying off current liabilities is one way management can lower its leverage ratio; in ABC's case, the current liabilities total $3,410,000.

This calculation involves totaling up all current assets except inventories and dividing that sum by the total current liabilities. The ratio should come to more than 1, which means that current assets exceed current liabilities. The larger the excess over 1, the more comfortable the margin. The acid test applied to a larger, more profitable company (and a real one), Halliburton, shows a ratio of 1.85.

In the case of ABC Metals, we divide $3,650,000 (the sum of cash, marketable securities, and receivables) by $3,410,000 (the total current liabilities), to arrive at a ratio of 1.07. This is not a very safe ratio, since it only slightly exceeds 1.

Now let's measure ABC's potential in terms of *the current ratio analysis*. Here we include in the calculations the value of the inventories on hand. This gives a longer-term picture of the company's position because it allows for the company to sell off its inventories in time. If the current ratio comes to a number greater than 1, the company will be able to meet all its current commitments.

To perform the current ratio analysis, you divide the total current assets by the total current liabilities. The numbers for ABC Metals are $8,440,000 divided by $3,410,000. The answer? 2.48.

That's pretty good. Halliburton's current ratio comes to 2.24. Given the inventories and the value of the work in progress, if push comes to shove, the company can floor-plan the operation—that is, borrow against inventories and work in progress.

Now for *the working-capital evaluation.* This is the number in which a friendly bank takes the greatest amount of interest if ABC Metals were to borrow against receivables and/or inventories. How much more short-term debt can the company assume without adding to the risk?

In this formula, we subtract total current liabilities ($3,410,000) from total current assets ($8,440,000). ABC Metals has a positive balance, a net figure of $5,030,000. That's not too shabby, either. This number represents the margin of safety that short-term creditors have in the current assets of the company.

So you see, an analysis of the balance sheet is one factor Fred can use in making an informed, though tentative, decision in favor of buying into his own company. The balance sheet passes all the tests through which it has been put.

Now, remember the discussion earlier about reporting assets at their cost? If we also consider that the assets are described in terms of original cost, not in terms of current market value, ABC's position is much better than it appears.

Still, before Fred can make a final decision, he has to look at two other documents: (1) the income statement and (2) the statement of changes in financial position (the funds-flow analysis).

Chapter 4

The Income Statement: The History of Operations

Whereas the balance sheet describes a company's financial position at a given moment in time, the income statement describes the operational process *over a period of time (usually one year).* In this statement, you can study the company's sales (revenues), costs, expenses, and profits or losses.

As in the case of the balance sheet, you should stop and look at words before lining them up with numbers. Please refer to the income statement shown earlier for ABC Metals.

The first consideration is sales. This refers to cash taken in from the sale of goods and/or services. If your company is in the business of manufacturing and selling widgets, then the money generated from the sale of those widgets we call *gross sales.* We include only those dollars that are acquired from ordinary operations and that we can expect the company to continue to produce.

A sale takes place when the title to the goods sold passes from the seller to the buyer, and the terms of the sale determine when that passage actually occurs.

The seller assumes the cost of freight if the terms for payment are free on board destination (FOB destination). Only when the goods reach their destination does title pass from seller to buyer. The seller therefore includes the cost of goods in his or her inventory and doesn't recognize the sale as revenue until the goods are accepted by the buyer. Anything still in transit when the balance sheet is written remains a part of the asset called inventory.

On the other hand, when the terms are FOB shipping point, the buyer assumes the cost of freight, and title passes to the buyer when the seller turns those goods over to the carrier. Now the seller takes the cost of the goods out of inventory and recognizes the gross sale price as revenue as soon as the carrier takes possession of them.

From gross sales we subtract out the discounts, any returns, and any allowances the firm may make; the result is net sales. Then, in order to show gross income (profit), we subtract the sum of the following expenses (which, altogether, are referred to as cost of goods sold) from net sales:

1. Cost of raw materials.
2. Cost of equipment and depreciation.
3. Cost of direct labor (wages of the people who actually perform the manufacturing process).

4. Cost of direct-labor benefits and insurance.
5. Cost of manufacturing overhead; for example, utilities.

In short, we deduct the costs of the factors of production—labor, facilities, equipment, and real estate.

We still have to deduct other expenses: *the cost of sales and the costs of general and administrative expenses.* The cost of sales includes advertising, commissions, salaries to salespeople, and the like. The overhead costs include salaries for managers and nonsales personnel, utilities other than those of the manufacturing plant, and so forth. The final tally is the *net income (or loss) from operations.*

But, no, we're not finished yet. There are transactions that produce gain or loss and that must be separately stated because they do not result from the normal operations of the business. An example of such a separate line item would be either gain or loss of sale on equipment. In addition, certain transactions are so important that they must be highlighted and called "extraordinary items." The criteria for calling a separate line item an extraordinary item are that the events that give rise to the gains and losses must be unusual in nature and infrequent in occurrence. An example of such an extraordinary item would be loss from damage due to an earthquake. After the separate line items are added in or subtracted out, what remains is the net income (or loss) before taxes.

That name tells you what comes next. Right. We subtract taxes—federal or state governmental income tax (if any)—from the net income (or loss) before taxes in order to come up with the bottom line: *net income (or loss) after taxes.* (Payroll, real estate, and sales taxes have already been taken into account in the body of the income statement.)

Chapter 5

Cost of Goods Sold, Overhead, and Profit

Just as I discussed the concept of the cost of assets, I need to pause here to discuss the ideas behind the cost of goods sold, overhead, and profit.

When we speak of cost of goods sold, we're distinguishing between that and the cost of goods produced whether or not they're sold. As I explained in an earlier chapter, only when goods are sold is their cost subtracted from sales. *The cost of unsold goods remains in finished-goods inventory until the goods are sold;* the company has merely replaced one asset (cash) with other assets (raw materials, labor, and so on), and those assets are then carried on the balance sheet rather than on the income statement until a sales transaction is made. Then the cost is matched against the sale, and the difference is the *gross income* (or *gross profit* or *gross margin*).

I've just applied the principle of *matching:* Revenues are matched with the cost of goods as they are sold.

Let's say that in the last year before ABC Metals removed itself from oil-field construction, it built three offshore rigs at a cost of $1 million each but sold only two of them, for $2 million each. We subtract just $2 million, not $3 million, from the income of $4 million. The gross income from those sales equals $2 million, and the balance sheet reflects a $1 million inventory of finished goods.

Not so with the general cost of operating the business: the cost of sales, general, and administrative overhead. Whereas we can match production costs with gross revenue from sales, we have no way of matching managers' salaries and other such indirect costs to each and every sale of produced goods. Therefore, we overlook the matching rule and expense certain indirect costs (for instance, insurance or advertising) over a period of several years.

In some service industries, however, it's possible to distribute overhead over a variety of services delivered. For example, in the consulting business or in social work in which each contract for services is negotiated separately, the administrative overhead can be factored into the contract itself, for the life of that contract, and records can be kept to reflect the services provided by the overhead elements. However, in the final income statement all separate contracts are combined.

What results from all these calculations is *the profit or loss picture of the operations during this year.* Yet the profit or loss doesn't depend exclusively on the sale of goods and/or services. Rather, when a company sells some of its assets, the result of that transaction gets factored in also. I referred to these as separate line items.

Most often, when a company sells off some of its assets, it doesn't recover the exact amount shown on the balance sheet for those assets. We call that amount the asset's *book value.*

Remember, I said that the balance sheet values the assets at original cost? Whereas we usually sell the finished-goods inventory at a price greater than original cost (thus showing a profit), we often sell plants, equipment, or property at less than book value.

Let's take that stamping machine I mentioned earlier. It's two years old, and technological advances have made it obsolete. A more efficient machine is available. Before ABC can buy the new one, it has to sell the old one.

Naturally, it won't sell the machine for a profit, for two reasons: (1) it's used, and (2) it's obsolete. Now, someone will buy it—for scrap or for a small machine shop somewhere—but ABC will recover only a portion of its cost. It will therefore show a loss in this transaction and subtract that loss from net income from operations.

As I've said before, accountants follow the principle of conservatism, which means that they would rather undervalue assets and income than run the risk of overvaluing them—and be accused of inflating the company's potential.

You can now see how that applies to the stamping—machine example. If ABC Metals sells off fixed assets at a loss, it can reasonably assume that future sell-offs will likewise bring in losses. On the other hand, selling off the adjacent property mentioned earlier at a profit may not be repeated in the future. After all, how many pieces of land does a company have to sell as compared to pieces of equipment? Remember that profits from other than normal operations and/or sales should always be disclosed separately in the income statement.

Chapter 6

Using the Income Statement and Balance Sheet Together

After all this, you're probably wondering about the connection between the income statement and the balance sheet. After you go back and take another look at the consolidated income statement of ABC Metals, shown in Chapter 1, I'll discuss how that information gets incorporated into the balance sheet, and the connection will become clear.

The two documents connect where the net income (or loss) of the income statement meets the retained earnings of the balance sheet. In the ABC example, the net income comes to $2,150,000. That net income is then added to the retained earnings on the previous year's balance sheet ($360,000). We then subtract any dividends distributed to the shareholders ($450,000), and the result is the balance now shown in retained earnings. And in this case, the result is quite substantial.

That good showing clearly marks a turnaround situation for ABC Metals. While the net income per share seems small ($0.430), the numbers suggest that this year's earnings are far superior to those in recent history. Of course, one way—probably the most critical way—to test the soundness of investing in this company is to look at the *return on equity (ROE)* that's beginning to emerge here.

Among the several measures of a company's profitability, the ROE is a special instance of *return on investment (ROI)*. The ROE identifies the return on the corporate equity or shareholders' investment. The higher the return, the better, and the minimum acceptable standard is .14 (14 percent). That means, when you divide net income after taxes by the equity, the result should be .14 or better.

In the case of ABC Metals, we divide $2,150,000 by $6,810,000, and the result is .31. Fred may have good reason to buy in, based on that number. ABC certainly is picking up.

But that's the *corporate* ROE. What about the shareholders' return on their personal equity (the *price-earnings ratio*)? You find that by dividing the market price per share by earnings per share. In this case, the earnings per share were $0.432. Let's say the market price per share is $1.60. The result? About 4. The price-earnings ratio determines whether the market price of a stock is reasonable or if it is too high or too low. In the case of ABC Metals, the price-earnings ratio seems reasonable.

The connection between the income statement and the balance sheet may become clearer if, for simplicity's sake, you assume that all transactions are for cash, with no receivable or payable accounts. Then, you follow these simple steps to reflect the changes from one year's balance sheet to the next:

1. In the balance sheet for this year, you increase cash by the net sales income.
2. Deduct the cost of goods actually sold from the inventory of finished goods on the previous balance sheet.
3. The cost of overhead decreases cash on hand by the same amount.
4. The sale of the stamping machine reduces the equipment category by the book value of the equipment, but adds the amount received to cash.
5. Finally, whatever taxes are paid reduce cash by that amount, and the balance sheet is balanced again.

Other ratios will help Fred determine whether or not he
wants to invest in ABC Metals. By analyzing the income
statement as well as the balance sheet, Fred can find a
variety of clear signals. First, we'll look at *asset turnover*
(activity) and then at *inventory turnover.*

To calculate asset turnover, Fred needs the beginning
balance of the company's current assets—that is, the current
assets as of April 30, 1984—as well as the assets as of April
30, 1985. He adds the beginning balance to the ending
balance, and divides the sum by 2. Then net sales is divided
by this number. That's the formula for asset turnover or
activity.

For the sake of illustration, I'll assume that those current
assets in 1984 were $7,000,000. Now, to determine the
activity during 1985, first add the beginning balance to the
ending balance, and then divide the result by 2: ($7,000,000
+ $8,440,000)/2 = $7,720,000. Next divide the net sales
figure from the income statement by the result:

$$7,335,000/7,720,000 = 95\%$$

That's a fair return on assets. However, just how good that
return is depends on a comparison—first, with other companies (such as Halliburton = 166 percent) and then with
this company's own previous performance. A high ratio
suggests an efficient use of assets; a low ratio implies the
opposite. Compared to its larger cousin, Halliburton, the
assets ratio doesn't look too good, but compared to ABC's
own record, that figure shows an improvement in management's use of company assets.

We can also judge management's efficiency in its use of
resources by calculating *inventory turnover.* To figure that,
divide the cost of sales by the average inventory for the year.
(You find the average inventory by dividing the sum of the
total value of inventory at the beginning of the year and at the
end of the year by 2.) The result shows you the number of
times inventory has "turned over" (that is, been produced
and sold) during the year. Usually, the higher the turnover
rate, the better.

Other measures taken from the income statement help
determine the efficiency of management, but those two

measures should be enough for now. You'll find the mc
important measures in the *statement of changes in financ*
position, or *funds analysis.*

Chapter 7

How to Evaluate
Management Decisions
Based on Financial Statements

Whenever you decide to buy or not to buy stock in a
company, you need to judge management efficiency. In fa
the buy decision should be based primarily on how well y
think management has performed in the past, how creative
has been, how much leadership it has shown. Those indic
tors at least suggest how well management will perform
the future. And it's your money management will be mana
ing.

Now, a *funds-flow analysis* helps you identify *the ma*
uses and sources of funds over time and determine wheth
those uses, or investments, result from appropriate source
For example, financing long-term investments from sho
term sources can prove dangerous. Consider the wisdom
financing a fixed asset such as a plant with a one-year ba
note. The wisdom of that decision depends on the willin
ness of the lenders to extend the note if payment can't l
made when the note is due. Even if the firm could pay tl
note on its due date, payment could leave it desperate
short of funds for other uses.

In order for you to understand how the funds-flow analys
helps you see what decisions management has made duri
the past period of operations, I need to go into more det
about the analysis; I need to define some more accounti
terms: *funds, sources of funds,* and *uses of funds.*

Funds means more than just cash. It refers to all financial resources: Cash is only one type of fund. Other types include credit and stockholders' equity.

A company can commit its resources by using cash or other means of payment, thereby changing the nature of its balance sheet by deploying resources to accounts in which investments are desired and by creatively financing its own purchases. The total process of resource deployment—using cash or other financial resources—is what is meant by use of funds.

GAAP require the use of the working capital definition of funds. Working capital is the excess of current assets over current liabilities. Working capital is a measurement of the safety factor for short-term creditors. Working capital may also be viewed as capital available for investment in noncurrent assets.

Use of funds is one classification of change in financial position. Any increase in noncurrent assets, as in the purchase of machinery; any decrease in noncurrent liabilities, as in retirement of a bond; and any decrease in owners' equity, as in ABC's operating deficits—these constitute uses of funds.

On the other hand, sources of funds include any decrease in noncurrent assets (for example, sale of machinery), any increase in long-term liabilities (for example, issuance of a bond), and any increase in owners' equity (for example, common stock).

We summarize all that with these four formulas:

1. An increase in a noncurrent asset = a use of funds.
2. A decrease in a noncurrent liability = a use of funds.
3. An increase in a noncurrent liability = a source of funds.
4. A decrease in a noncurrent asset = a source of funds.

And once more you can see how changes in assets and liabilities balance each other:

Any change in an asset or a liability produces an equal change in the other; for instance, borrowing money increases cash, an asset (a use of funds), while increasing liabilities (notes payable—a source of funds).

A company can reduce owners' equity either by operating losses or by repurchasing shares from shareholders. In the case of equity reduced by operating losses, if the company begins to buy up shares from present owners (as, for example, Phillips Petroleum Company has recently done), the number of shares will remain the same, but in all likelihood the market value of the shares will decrease, thereby reducing the shareholders' equity even further. The situation, in either case, shows a negative change—a drain of funds from the total of funds. Only by using funds—that is, only by investing them—does a firm increase assets or reduce liabilities.

When drawing on the sources of funds, a firm increases owners' equity with the profits of operations or with the sale of new stock (or any other way of adding capital as opposed to operating profits). There are various sources of funds; for example, a company may decide to decrease assets by selling outright assets it doesn't really need, or it might opt to reduce its level of investments in securities. Or if the firm gets more credit from banks (increasing its payables) or gets deferred tax credit from the government or otherwise adds to its credit balances, it is receiving resources from outside sources for running its business.

Since I've been talking about increases and decreases you've figured out by now that a *funds-flow analysis is comparative statement.* You start by comparing beginning and ending balances, as I did earlier when I talked about asset turnover and inventory turnover. Then, you identify the sources and uses of funds described above by drawing information from both the balance sheets and the income statements for the periods being examined. The format of the funds-flow analysis, a sample of which appears in the accompanying sidebar, makes it possible for you to see major sources and uses of funds that the other documents can't disclose as readily.

When you study a *statement of changes in financial position,* as you would if investing in a company, you need instruments from several different time periods—at least from this year and last year. The variations you see will show you just how efficient or inefficient management has been

That's particularly true of changes in retained earnings, in net property, and in net cash from operations.

When analyzing retained earnings, whether the figure reflects an increase or a decrease, you have to check to see if the total income listed on the funds-flow statement includes cash dividends to the shareholders. The net income figure on the income statement serves you better as a source of funds than as a use of them. The dividend distribution is better cataloged as an outflow of funds (a use of funds).

You will also want to see the changes in net property. Do the changes result from sales from the gross fixed-property accounts, or from accumulated depreciaiton, or from retirement of plant and equipment? Or are the changes the result of all those combined? Obviously, changes from the sale of fixed property could increase the availability of funds for other purposes more dramatically than could the increases from other changes.

The net cash from operations—that's the bottom line you keep hearing about. If you reexamine the outline in the sidebar on pages 36–37, you'll see that write-offs—noncash expenses—increase funds from operations: depreciation of plant and equipment, amortization of patents or copyrights, or other intangible assets. These figures tell you the actual cash position of the company better than either the balance sheet or the income statement.

Still, no accounting document is ever perfectly clear or accurate. That's why it's also important to know the accounting principles (GAAP) reflected by the statement and to read the footnotes in any statement.

Outline of a Typical Statement of Changes in
Financial Position

Funds from operations:

Income from operations
Add items not affecting funds (that is, income other than
from sales)
Depreciation
Amortization of intangibles
Deferred federal income taxes
Deferred compensation
Other charges (such as gain or loss from sale of an
investment)
TOTAL FROM OPERATIONS (which number will be
larger than the net income figure on the income
statement)

Changes in:

Accounts receivable (an increase if the comparison be-
tween beginning and ending balances yields a negative
number; a decrease if the number is positive)
Inventories (the same analysis applies)
Prepaid expenses (the same analysis applies)
Accounts payable (an increase if the comparison between
beginning and ending balances yields a positive number; a decrease if the number is negative)
Accrued expenses (the same analysis applies)
Accrued taxes (the same analysis applies)
NET CASH FROM OPERATIONS (= the sum of the
total from operations and the total from the changes
listed immediately above)

Financing and investment activity:

Increases in long-term debt
Less decreases in long-term debt
Proceeds from the sale of stock or bonds
Proceeds from the sale of an investment
Less cash dividends
Less cost of purchase of other securities

Less cost of discretionary purchases (for example, property, plant, and equipment)

Other (such as decrease or increase in investment from discontinued operations)

Working capital items other than cash equivalents (a negative number indicates an increase; a positive number, a decrease):

Trade accounts and notes receivable
Unbilled costs and inventories
Short-term debt
Trade accounts payable
Wages or benefits accrued
Advance payments by customers
Income taxes

- -

Chapter 8

Accounting Principles and Footnotes: The Heart of the Matter

You've seen considerable discussion of the *principle of cost* and the *principle of matching.* You're familiar with the *principle of conservatism*—the accountants' tendency, wherever possible, to choose an accounting method that portrays a company's financial picture in the least favorable light—and you should also become conversant with several other principles: namely, the *principle of realization,* the *principle of consistency,* the *principle of consolidation,* and the *principle of materiality.* These principles give more meaning to the annual report than any of management's claims or promises, and they control how the 10K statement I described earlier is written.

Let's linger on the *principle of conservatism* for a moment. I mentioned that the accountants' choice of method protects the investor from being falsely or overly optimistic concerning a company's performance. Better to be pessimistic, economists and accountants say. That's probably one reason why they call economics "the dismal science."

Actually, a sound business reason underlies the principle of conservatism. All companies run risks that should be reflected in the accounting process as best they can be. Losses or expenses, even if the firm is not certain how much they'll be, should appear on the statements. These include bad debts, potential claims against insurance, and so forth. Contingent liabilities (liabilities that may or may not come into existence) should be disclosed in the footnotes. The inclusion of these items makes the risks to the investor exceedingly clear.

At the same time, by not including on the statements *possible* as opposed to *actual* gains, the firm recognizes that promises don't always pay off as often as threats. A financial statement of a going concern that includes a whole lot of promises has something to hide. (That's not true of a start-up situation. A start-up operation has little more than promises to offer.)

You can probably see a connection between the principle of cost I described earlier in the book and this principle of conservatism. Since the only value of property, equipment, raw materials, and so on of which a company can be perfectly sure is the price it paid, it follows that by showing only its original cost, the firm is adhering to the principle of conservatism as well. It doesn't really know if its assets are appreciating until it actually sells them for a profit.

On the other hand, if an asset has depreciated, and the company knows it has, as in the case of that stamping machine, the principle of conservatism forces the firm to reflect that depreciation when recognizing the value of a fixed asset.

That brings us to the *principle of realization.* This refers to the way a company reports its sales and thereby its profits. By virtue of a specified point at which a profit is made, or *realized,* we can compare the accounting reports of different companies and of the same company at different times. That's what I was talking about when I discussed the question of when the consumer takes title to the goods—FOB shipping point or FOB destination.

That type of information should be declared in the footnotes of the statements so you can tell the true value of the inventories and of the income from goods sold.

The footnote on recognition should also specify whether or not revenues recognized as income are from any sources other than from goods sold—for instance, from rentals as they accrue or from services when they are performed. The footnote should also explain how revenues are recorded from sales on long-term contracts—for example, as a percentage of completion, whereby income is recognized based on the estimated state of completion of individual contracts.

Closely related to realization is the *principle of consolidation.* What does the statement include? A statement should include all business conducted by the organization during the period covered. The footnote should also specify whether or not the statement includes gains and losses from foreign currency transactions and translation.

What's included on a statement should be significant. The *principle of materiality* allows an accountant to overlook small expenses, such as a piece of inexpensive office furniture—unless, of course, such expenses are significant to that particular business. It follows, therefore, that what's significant to ABC Metals may not be significant to Halliburton.

However else the financial statements are stated, they must be stated consistently. The *principle of consistency* demands that once a company has chosen a particular method for accounting for its assets and liabilities, it should stick with it—unless necessity requires a change in accounting methods. The following guidelines should be used by a firm when making a change, and if they are not used, then you should consider the firm's reports—and perhaps also its motives—suspect.

1. The change should be a response to a permanent and irreversible change in the way the company conducts business (such as a change in reporting inventory) or in business conditions (such as the real scarcity of a commodity that forces up the price permanently).
2. The change should be reported in the year in which it is made. The change and its effect on income should be disclosed appropriately.
3. The accounting reports from previous years should be updated to reflect the changes, thereby making all reports compatible.

These fundamental principles of accounting govern all production of financial statements. The body of generally accepted accounting principles is very much more extensive than this, of course, as the AICPA and its Accounting Principles Board and, more recently, the FASB have established a great number of rules that stem from these principles. Nevertheless, no single set of accounting principles rules the world of the CPA.

Business itself makes a single set of rules impossible. The diversity of businesses requires a diversity of principles rather than one uniform principle for all businesses for all time. That one uniform principle, if applied universally, could confuse or mislead rather than assist rational decision making.

Managers or investors need to know the basic principles of accounting, but they also need to know how to apply them on an individual basis to a specific industry. They also need to be aware of the special rules that apply strictly to their own business—as with the insurance industry, which has to distinguish very carefully between types of income (premium versus investment) and allocated reserves and their uses.

Only by studying the statements found at the end of annual reports or in 10Ks can you make the proper decision for yourself with respect to buying or not buying into an organization. Only by studying these statements can you see the role you play in the growth and development of the company. By comparing these statements with the plans that management has announced for the company, you can test whether or not that management is successful as well as efficient.

Chapter 9

How to Understand Management-Control Reports

Another place in which to find financial statements is a company's business plan, especially if it's a privately held company into which you're thinking of buying. Just as important as those financials, the projections over a period of time—say, five years—tell you about the efficiency of management. Comparison between actual performance and the plan also tells you whether or not the company is successful in realizing the targets it has set for itself, and whether it is doing so in the time specified.

Every well-run company has a strategic plan that spells out the targets the management intends to achieve, the deadlines for when they'll be achieved, and the means that will be used to achieve them. To control the implementation of that plan, we have the *management-control report,* tne most important part of which, for our purposes, is the budget. It states how much money the managers expect to make, how they intend to use funds, and what sources they expect to tap to generate funds.

Check out your own company to see whether or not it has a management-control report with at least a budget from which to operate and a way of generating information that allows you to compare actual performance with the plan. There should also be a system that allows the firm to take corrective action when reality deviates from ideal.

Let's stick with the manufacturing example. It's the easiest to formulate.

The budget of a manufacturing firm should include projections for both variable and fixed costs as well as a target for production. The target should be expressed as an output—as a number of units to be produced in a given period of time.

For each year, the plan should target a specified number of units.

The cost of producing the total output in one year is then projected by adding together the following variable factors:

Direct labor
Direct materials
Manufacturing overhead

By dividing that total by the total output, the per-unit manufacturing cost can be computed.

But you'll probably remember that I said that general, administrative, and sales costs can't be computed that specifically. Instead we break out costs in terms of assumed fixed and assumed variable factors. The assumed fixed costs include:

Indirect labor (such as secretarial support)
Maintenance
Depreciation
Property and other taxes
Supervision
Office expenses

Costs we assume to be variable include:

Indirect materials (such as lubricants for machinery)
Tooling
Utilities and telephone

In a management-control report, we take the sum of all these factors, divide that by total output, and arrive at a per-unit cost of overhead. However, most companies don't bother to consider that in their final financial reports. This information is a management tool, not an investment measure.

As time elapses, actual performance figures are entered into the report to show with actual monthly and year-to-date figures how well the company is doing relative to its plan. If any deviations from plan show up—such as income being lower than expected or costs being higher—corrective steps can be taken before the deviations get out of hand. And those actual figures in the management-control report then get transferred to the firm's monthly income statements.

I've deliberately oversimplified the process of budget management because the actual details are much too gruesome for this type of study. However, I've included this much in the present discussion because budget management is an essential part of effective business management.

When analyzing financial statements, you should look not only at the balance sheet, the income statement, and the statement of changes in financial position; you should also look into how close to plan the managers have been. The financials might look great on the surface, but they could also reflect the fact that management has not fulfilled the wishes of the board of directors or the shareholders. The managers may have conducted a good bit of business, but was it the right business—the business the investors hired it to conduct?

Chapter 10

Conclusion: The Bottom Line

I've been trying to take out some of the mumbo jumbo found in most accountants' reports. *Assets, liabilities, equity, leverage*—words most people find a bit too arcane for their taste.

Yet those words refer to pieces of information that dramatically affect your life. That language describes how your salary is paid and whether or not you can afford a mortgage for a new home or afford to finance a small business. For all their limitations, financial statements describe the real world of business and economics better than any other document can.

You need to read financial statements if you want to know where you are financially and how you got there—and then plan where you want to get to from here.

To buy a car on credit, you need to provide the bank with a personal statement of net worth (also called a personal financial statement). That's a personal balance sheet, a sample of which is shown in the accompanying sidebar.

Sample Statement of Personal Net Worth

ASSETS		LIABILITIES	
Cash on hand	$ 5,000	Debts	
Convertible bonds or securities	50,000	Mortgage	$ 70,000
		Automobile 1	6,500
Other assets, such as houses, automobiles, paid-up insurance, furniture, appliances	160,000	Automobile 2	5,250
		Other loans, such as mortgage on rental property	10,000
TOTAL ASSETS	$ 215,000	TOTAL LIABILITIES	$ 91,750
		NET WORTH (Total assets less liabilities)	$ 123,250

To invest money in business ventures, you need to understand the business plan, which contains balance sheets, income statements, and projected budgets (income and expenses).

To determine how well its managers are conducting a company's business, you need to be able to analyze the data on the balance sheets, the income statements, the statements of changes in financial position, and the budgets of the management-control report.

To grasp the impact of current events on your life—such as friendly or unfriendly takeovers or mergers—you need to understand what the financial commentators are saying when they talk about the relative values of the companies involved or the values of the offers.

Financial statements describe the economic value of an individual, a company, or a social institution. That means they express value in terms of money.

A balance sheet describes where a firm is at a given point in time. It condenses its entire economic history into one statement of assets and liabilities. It describes what the company owns (assets) and how much what it owns is worth

It describes what the firm owes (liabilities) and how much what it owes costs—its debt.

It also describes what the owners of a company have coming to them. Whether they are sole proprietors, partners, or shareholders, the money they invest in a company belongs to them—plus, hopefully, a net profit. Therefore, a business has a dual obligation to its owners: (1) to protect their initial investment and (2) to increase the owners' net worth. The balance sheet shows just how well the company's management fulfills both obligations.

The income statement describes how the firm got what it owns or owes. It describes the organization's economic activity over a period of time. It describes sales (revenues) and what resources the firm used to make those sales. From those figures, the company's profit (income) or loss can be computed. That final figure then gets added into the firm's equity—what it has left over if it doesn't remove the money from the business in the form of dividends or liquidation.

To see just how well a particular business's management team performs its obligation, you can read the statement of changes in financial position, or the funds-flow analysis. That document compares the current financial resources of the company with its resources at the beginning of the reporting period. Naturally, any increase in assets and reduction in liabilities speak well for the firm's managers. On the other hand, you should raise questions if the situation is reversed.

Many of these questions can be answered by reading the footnotes of financial documents. Sometimes the principles of accounting themselves can make an otherwise reasonable situation seem bleak.

The principle of conservatism always paints a relatively pessimistic picture in order to underscore the risks involved in doing business.

The principle of recognition will only take into account sales when completed.

The principle of matching allows a company to show only the costs of goods actually sold.

The principle of cost permits a firm to show assets only on the basis of acquisition costs, and if assets have appreciated, that increase in value will be ignored.

Finally, management performance must be judged also on the basis of how well the company's plans are being fulfilled. Any owners of a profit-making business should still consider whether or not the profits they show are the profits they set out to earn. If not, then steps can be taken to shore up the operations of the business.

Well, then, the bottom line to all this is that while by now you're no accountant, you should be in a better position to understand what the accountants are trying to tell you.

Glossary

Accounting methods: The two ways to report sales and expenses. Cash method = reporting sales when cash is received and reporting expenses when cash is paid. Accrual method = reporting income and expenses as they are incurred, whether or not cash is paid or received.

Assets: Anything of value owned by the company and to which the company possesses clear title (tangible and intangible items included); the economic resources the company owns. Current assets = resources that the company expects to use in a short period of time. Fixed assets = property, plant, or equipment used in the operations of the business, usually having a life of several years.

Balance sheet: A cross-sectional view of a company's financial position that lists a company's assets, liabilities, and equity at a given point in time.

Bonds: Instruments of long-term debt sold to investors, with a fixed rate of interest and an agreed-upon due date.

Book value: (1) the dollar amount of an asset recorded in the company's ledgers; its net value. (2) The value of the common shareholders' equity divided by the number of shares of common stock outstanding. (3) The base buy-in value of a partner's share of a privately held company. (See also *paid-in capital*.)

Capital stock: Certificates of ownership sold to investors by a corporation, which certificates entitle their owners not only to a share of the profits but also to other privileges, depending upon the type of stock purchased.

Cash-flow statement: A statement of cash inflows and outflows that includes other financing and investment activities; it may be used as a barometer of a company's financial strength.

Common shares: The class of stock that entitles the bearers to share in all the basic rights of owning stock, especially the right to vote for the board of directors. (See also *paid-in capital, par value,* and *preferred shares*.)

Floor planning: Borrowing money against inventories in order to solve a cash-flow problem.

Funds: All resources available to a company for use in operations, including credit and other forms of borrowed money.

Generally accepted accounting principles (GAAP): The basic concepts from which all accounting rules adopted by the AICPA and FASB stem. The purpose of GAAP is to permit comparison of financial statements. Several of the most important principles are:

1. *Conservatism:* Portraying a company's financial picture in the least favorable light, wherever possible.
2. *Matching:* Pairing any income with the costs incurred in the process of generating it.
3. *Cost:* Recording the value of assets at their original cost until they are sold or otherwise liquidated.
4. *Realization:* Including on the income statement only those revenues that are earned, that is, where a sales transaction has been completed or a service performed.
5. *Consolidation:* Specifying what the statement includes—usually all the business conducted by the organization during the period covered.
6. *Consistency:* Using the same method of accounting throughout all a company's statements.

7. *Materiality:* Overlooking small expenses unless those expenses are significant to the conduct of business.

Income statement: The document that shows the company's financial operations over a period of time, reporting all revenues and expenses.

Leveraging: Borrowing money to operate the company or to buy out shares in the company.

Liabilities: Money, goods, or services owed by the company. Current liabilities = short-term debts (payable within one year) and other immediate demands on resources such as accounts payable. Long-term liabilities = debt payable in more than one year, such as loans or bonds.

Owners' (shareholders') equity: The total book value of the shares held by investors in the company; the sum of the value of the preferred stock, the total par value of the common stock plus the paid-in capital plus the retained earnings; the shareholders' claims against the resources of the company.

Paid-in capital: That portion of stockholders' equity that was invested or paid in by stockholders as opposed to capital generated by the company.

Par value: The original value of the stock when it is offered to the public (usually $1.00 to $1.25 per share).

Preferred shares: Certificates of ownership that entitle the bearers to first claim against company assets in the event of the company's failure, in exchange for which right the bearers yield most other shareholder rights (especially voting rights).

Profit: What's left over after costs of goods sold, expenses, and taxes are deducted from sales and revenues.

Ratio analyses: Financial statistics used to measure companies against each other and against industry standards. The main ratios are:

1. *Leverage ratio analysis:* The relationship of total liabilities to shareholders' equity is found by dividing total liabilities by the total shareholders' equity. This shows how much of the company's ability to conduct business comes from borrowed funds (that is, the extent to which it is leveraged).

2. *Acid test:* A method for gauging the company's liquidity, its ability to convert assets into cash and/or meet its short-term commitments. The sum of all current assets except inventories is divided by total current liabilities. A ratio of 1 or better is the accepted minimum standard.

3. *Current ratio analysis:* A longer-term picture of the company's ability to meet its commitments. This includes inventories in the calculations along with other current assets. The resulting figure is then divided by total current liabilities. The greater the number in excess of 1, the better the picture.

4. *Working-capital evaluation:* A measure of risk to investors if the company is considering adding to its borrowed funds. Total current liabilities are subtracted from total current assets to determine the margin of safety a creditor has in the current assets of the company.

5. *Return on equity:* A special instance of return on investment in which the ratio identifies the return on the corporate equity or shareholders' investment. Net income after taxes (in the year under consideration) is divided by equity to determine corporate ROE.

6. *Price-earnings ratio:* The ROE on shareholders' investment. Earnings per share are divided by the market price per share of common stock.

7. *Asset turnover:* The return on assets, a method for determining if assets are used productively. The balance of total assets at the beginning of the year is added to the balance of total assets at the end of the year and divided by 2; then net sales is divided by the result. The higher the percentage, the better the performance.

8. *Inventory turnover:* Another method of measuring management efficiency. The cost of sales is divided by the average inventory during the year. (Average inventory = the sum of the total value of the inventory at the beginning of the year and at the end of the year divided by 2.)

Retained earnings: That portion of the company's accumulated profits that has not been distributed to the owners and is carried on the books.

Sales (revenue): Cash received for the sale of goods and/or services. Gross sales = the total value of sales. Net sales = the value of sales after returns and allowances have been subtracted.

Statement of changes in financial position: A comparative statement of the uses and sources of funds over time; a statement of changes in financial position helps an investor determine whether those uses, or investments, result from appropriate sources—that is, whether or not management has made proper use of its resources.

10K report: Documents required annually by the Securities and Exchange Commission, that accurately describe the company's financial position, including balance sheets, income statements, statements of changes in financial position, inventories, pension plans, and so on.

Bibliography

"How to Analyze Accounting Reports." *Executive Skills*, a monthly publication of the American Management Association (New York), Vol. II, No. 79–11 (November 1979), pp. 1–16.

"How to Interpret Financial Statements." *Executive Skills*, op. cit., Vol. VII, No. 84–86 (June 1984), pp. 1–16.

Kristy, James E., and Diamond, Susan Z. *Finance Without Fear.* New York: AMACOM, 1984.

Index

About the Author

Donald H. Weiss is an Account Executive for Psychological Associates, a training and development company, and President of Self-Management Associates, a small-business consulting firm located in Dallas. Along with the six books in the Successful Office Skills series, he has written numerous books, articles, video scripts, and study guides on business management and related topics. Dr. Weiss is the author of AMACOM's popular cassette/workbook programs *Getting Results, How to Manage for Higher Productivity,* and *Managing Conflict.*

Dr. Weiss holds a Ph.D. in social theory from Tulane University, as well as degrees from the University of Arizona and the University of Missouri. He has also taught at several colleges and universities. He is a member of the American Society for Training and Development.